30

A 30-DAY DEVOTIONAL TREASURY

CHARLES SPURGEON

Prayer

COMPILED AND EDITED BY

LANCE WUBBELS

Emerald Books
P.O. Box 635
Lynnwood, WA 98046

Emerald Books are distributed through YWAM Publishing. For a full list of titles, including other devotionals and classics, visit our website at www.ywampublishing.com or call 1-800-922-2143.

10 09 08 07 06   10 9 8 7 6 5 4 3 2

Published by Emerald Books
P.O. Box 635
Lynnwood, WA 98046

ISBN 1-883002-96-6

Printed in Colombia.

30-Day Devotional Treasuries Series

Introduction

Considered by his peers then and now as "The Prince of Preachers," Charles Spurgeon built London's Metropolitan Tabernacle into the world's largest independent congregation during the nineteenth century. Much has been made of the combination of a beautiful speaking voice, a dramatic flair and style that was captivating, a powerful commitment to a biblical theology, and his ability to speak to the people of his day in a manner that addressed their deepest needs. But the foremost secret that empowered Spurgeon was his devotion to prayer.

When people would walk through the Metropolitan Tabernacle, Spurgeon would take them to the basement prayer room where people were always on their knees interceding for the church.

Then Spurgeon would declare, "Here is the power-house of this church." This statement was backed by the amazing number of sermons that he preached on prayer.

Spurgeon was a great believer and teacher in passionate, Holy Spirit–directed prayer. He paints masterful, passionate word pictures that are marvelously instructive on the theme of prayer.

Well over one hundred years have gone by since Spurgeon's voice echoed through his great London church. But time has in no way diminished the powerful effect of Spurgeon's words. I invite you to read these thirty devotionals as you would listen to a trusted and skilled pastor. Careful editing has helped to sharpen the focus of these readings while retaining the authentic and timeless flavor they undoubtedly bring.

Knock!

—∞∞∞—

"Ask and it will be given to you;
seek and you will find; knock and the
door will be opened to you."
—MATTHEW 7:7

Let us abound in prayer. Nothing under heaven pays like prevailing prayer. He who has power in prayer has all things at his call.

Ask for everything you need, whatever it may be: if it is a good and right thing, it is promised to the sincere seeker. Seek for what Adam lost you by the Fall, and for what you have lost yourself by neglect, by your backsliding, by your lack of prayer. Seek till you find the grace you need. Then knock. If you seem shut out from comfort, from knowledge, from hope, from God, then knock; for the Lord will open it to you. Here you need the Lord's own intervention: you can ask and receive, you can seek and find; but you cannot knock and open—the Lord must Himself open the door, or you are shut out forever. God is ready to open the door. There is no cherub with fiery sword to guard this gate, but, on the contrary, the Lord Jesus Himself opens and no man shuts.

If you seem shut out from comfort, from knowledge, from hope, from God, then knock; for the Lord will open it to you.

Do you fear that sin has barred the gate of grace shut? Your desponding feelings fasten up the door in your judgment. Yet, it is not so. The gate is not barred or bolted as you think it is. Though it may be spoken of as closed in a certain sense, yet in another sense it is never shut. In any case it opens very freely; its hinges are not rusted, no bolts secure it. The Lord is glad to open the gate to every knocking soul. It is closed far more in your apprehension than as a matter of fact. Have faith and enter at this moment through holy courage.

And if we plead with God for a while without realized success, it makes us more earnest. David pictured himself as sinking in the miry clay, lower and lower, till he cried out of the depths, and then at last he was taken up out of the horrible pit, and his feet were set on a rock. So, our hearts need enlarging. The spade of agony is digging trenches to hold the water of life. If the ships of prayer do not come home speedily, it is because they are more heavily freighted with blessing. If you knock with a heavy heart, you shall yet sing with joy of spirit. Never be discouraged!

———⊸⊷⊶———

Lord Jesus, You alone can open the door that I am knocking on. Come to me, I pray. Amen.

Do Not Worry

⚯

*"Therefore I tell you, do not worry about your life,
what you will eat or drink; or about your body, what you will
wear. Is not life more important than food, and the body more
important than clothes? Look at the birds of the air..."*
—MATTHEW 6:25–26

U ndue anxiety is very common among us. Certain of us are nervous, timid, doubtful, and prone to fear. There are plenty of pessimists about, although they will hardly recognize themselves by that title. To them evil is always impending; we are about to take a leap in the dark. All their birds are owls or ravens. All their swans are black. If it rains today, it will rain tomorrow, and the next, and the next, and in all probability there will be a deluge. Or if it is a fine day today, it will be dry tomorrow, and so on for months, until the earth and all the meadows perish with drought. I suppose they cannot help it, but Christians must help it. For the Lord's word is plain and binding: "Do not worry about your life."

Fretful anxiety is forbidden for the believer, and it is needless. If you have a Father in heaven to care for you, are you not put to shame by every little bird that sits upon the bough and sings, though it has not two grains of barley in all the world? God takes charge of the birds of the air, and thus they live exempt from care; why don't we?

Prudence is wisdom, for it adapts means to ends; but anxiety is folly, for it groans and worries, and accomplishes nothing.

Our Lord also taught that such anxiety is useless, for, with all our care, we cannot add a single hour to our life. Can we do anything else by fretful care? What if the farmer deplores that there is no rain? Do his fears unstop the bottles of heaven? It is infinitely wiser to do our best, and then cast our care upon our God. Prudence is wisdom, for it adapts means to ends; but anxiety is folly, for it groans and worries, and accomplishes nothing.

Besides, "the pagans run after all these things." Let the heir of heaven act a nobler part than the mere man of the world. Our distrust of our God is childish and dishonoring. If we could not trust Him, could we manage better ourselves? Can we do better than "know that in all things God works for the good of those who love him"?

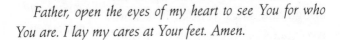

Father, open the eyes of my heart to see You for who You are. I lay my cares at Your feet. Amen.

DAY 3

Adoption:
The Spirit and the Cry

———∞∞∞———

*Because you are sons, God sent the Spirit
of his Son into our hearts, the Spirit
who calls out, "Abba, Father."*
—GALATIANS 4:6

The word *Abba* is of all words in all languages
the most natural word for father. It is truly a
child's word; and I have no doubt that our Master
felt, in His Gethsemane agony, a love for child's
words (Mark 14:36). I think this sweet word *Abba*
was chosen to show us that we are to be very natural with God, not stilted and formal. We are to be
very affectionate, to come close to Him and be bold
to lie in His bosom, looking up into His face and

speaking with holy boldness. "Abba" is not a word, somehow, but a babe's lisping. Oh, how near we are to God when we can use such speech! How dear He

What child minds his father hearing him cry?

is to us and dear we are to Him when we may say to Him, like the great Son Himself, "Abba, Father."

The cry in our hearts is not only childlike, but the tone and manner of utterance are equally so. Note that it is a *cry*. If we obtain an audience with a king, we do not cry; we speak in meas-

ured tones and set phrases. But the Spirit of God takes away the formality, leading us to cry "Abba." Even our very cries are full of the spirit of adoption. And what child minds his father hearing him cry? When the Spirit in us sends forth cries and groans, we are not ashamed, nor are we afraid to cry before God. Perhaps you think that God will not hear your prayers because you cannot pray grandly like some other person. But the Spirit of His Son cries, and you cannot do better than cry, too. Be satisfied to offer to God broken language, words salted with your griefs, wetted with your tears. Go to Him with holy familiarity and be not afraid to cry in His presence, "Abba, Father."

Has He not brought us so near to Him that sometimes we say, "I will not let you go unless you bless me" (Gen. 32:26)? We cry after Him, our heart and our flesh cry out for God, for the living God.

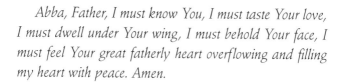

Abba, Father, I must know You, I must taste Your love, I must dwell under Your wing, I must behold Your face, I must feel Your great fatherly heart overflowing and filling my heart with peace. Amen.

Effectual Prayer

———⊷⊷⊷———

*"As soon as you began to pray, an answer
was given, which I have come to tell you,
for you are highly esteemed."*
—DANIEL 9:23

To what shall I liken the pleadings of Daniel? It seems to me as though he thundered and lightninged at the gate of heaven. He stood there before God and said, "O Most High, You have brought me to this place as You brought Jacob to the Jabbok, and with You all night I mean to stay and wrestle till the break of day. I cannot and will not let You go unless You bless me." No prayer is at all likely to bring down an immediate answer if it is not a fervent prayer. "The effectual fervent prayer of a righteous man availeth much" (James 5:16 KJV), but if it is not fervent, we cannot expect to find it effectual. We must get rid of the icicles that hang about our lips. We must ask the Lord to thaw the ice caves of our soul and make our hearts like a furnace of fire heated seven times hotter. If our hearts do not burn within us, we may well question whether Jesus is with us. Those who are neither cold nor hot He has threatened to spew out of His mouth (Rev. 3:16). If He is "a consuming fire," He will not commune with us until our souls grow to be like consuming fires, too.

No prayer is at all likely to bring down an immediate answer if it is not a fervent prayer.

Oh, for a mighty cry! A prevailing cry! A heaven-shaking cry! A cry that would make the gates of heaven open! A cry that God's arm could not resist! A cry of saints knit together in love and filled with holy passion! Let God throw the stone into the stagnant pool of His church, and I can see the waves of revival going out all around the world. God's kingdom will spread, and days of refreshing will come from the presence of the Lord. Let us now say in His sight that even if He does not please to hear us at the beginning of the supplication, it is our desire to wait upon Him until He does. You still remain hidden behind the mountains, yet we wait for You as they that wait for the morning. But tarry not, O our God! Make haste our Beloved.

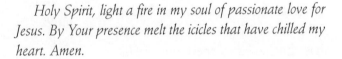

Holy Spirit, light a fire in my soul of passionate love for Jesus. By Your presence melt the icicles that have chilled my heart. Amen.

Praying in the Spirit

⸻∞⸻

Pray in the Holy Spirit.
—JUDE 20

It is a delightful reflection that God observes His
people and does not sit as an indifferent spectator
of their conflicts and difficulties. The Lord knows
our frailties and failures in prayer, yet He is not
angry with us. Instead, He is moved to pity us and
to love us. Instead of shutting the gates of mercy, He
devises ways to bring the lame into His presence. He
teaches the ignorant how to pray and strengthens
the weak with His own strength. That help is not
found in a book or in the repetition of certain words

in certain consecrated places, but in the condescending assistance of the Holy Spirit.

I understand that the Holy Spirit is actually willing to help me pray, that He will tell me how to pray, and that when I get to a point where I am at a loss for words and cannot express my desires, He will appear in my extremity and make intercession in me with groanings that cannot be uttered. Jesus in His Gethsemane agony was strengthened by an angel; you are to be strengthened by God Himself. This thought needs no adorning of oratorical expression. Take it as a wedge of gold of Ophir and value it; it is priceless, beyond all price. God the Holy Ghost condescends to assist you when you are on your knees, and if you cannot put two words together in common speech to men, yet He will help you speak with God. And if at the mercy seat you fail in words, you will not fail in reality, for your heart shall conquer. God requires no words. He never reads our petitions according to the outward

> *If at the mercy seat you fail in words, you will not fail in reality, for your heart shall conquer.*

expression but reads them according to the inward groaning. He notices the longing, the desiring, the sighing, the crying.

Remember that the outward of prayer is but the shell; the inward prayer is its true kernel and essence. Indeed, a prayer wailed forth in the bitter anguish from a desolate spirit—a cry so discordant to human ears—is music to the ear of God. Notice the value of the heart in prayer and be comforted.

—⁂—

Holy Spirit, teach me to pray, strengthen me to pray. My heart is Yours. Intercede for me before the Father's throne. Amen.

True Prayer, True Power

—————— ⚭ ——————

*"Therefore I tell you, whatever you
ask for in prayer, believe that you have
received it, and it will be yours."*
—MARK 11:24

Look upward, and let us weep. O God, You have given us a mighty weapon, and we have permitted it to rust. You have given us that which is as mighty as Yourself, and we have let that power lie dormant. What must we say of ourselves when God has given us power in prayer—matchless power, full of blessedness to ourselves, and of unnumbered mercies to others—and yet that power lies still. To Your people You have given a gift that is better than the sun or wind or life, and yet we permit it to lie still. We almost forget that we even wield the power. Weep, believer. We have been defeated and our banners trail in the dust because we have not prayed. Go back to your God and confess before Him that you were armed and carried bows but turned your back in the day of battle. Your spirit has not been moved. Wake up, wake up, and be astonished: you have neglected prayer. Wrestle and strive with your God, and the blessing shall come—

I challenge you to exceed in prayer the Master's bounty.

the early and the latter rain of His mercy, and the earth shall bring forth plenteously, and all the nations shall call Him blessed.

Once more, look up and rejoice. You have not sought His face, but behold He cries to you still, "Seek my face." What a blessed thing it is that the Master in heaven is always ready to hear! Let every vein of your heart be full to the brim with the rich blood of desire, and struggle and wrestle and strive with God for it, using the promises and pleading the attributes of God, and see if God does not give you your heart's desire. I challenge you to exceed in prayer the Master's bounty. Believe Him to be more than He is. Open your mouth so wide that He cannot fill it. Go to Him now for more faith than the promise warrants. Venture it, risk it, outdo the Eternal if it is possible. See if through believing Him, He does not fulfill the promise and richly bless you with the anointing oil of His Spirit by which you will be strong in prayer. He will hear you, and you shall yet pray as prevailing princes.

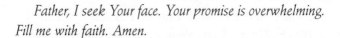

Father, I seek Your face. Your promise is overwhelming. Fill me with faith. Amen.

Unceasing Prayer

—✖—

Pray continually.
—1 THESSALONIANS 5:17

O ur Lord Jesus Christ in these words assures you that you may pray without ceasing. There is no time when you may not pray. There is not one unholy moment in the hour, nor one unaccepted hour in the day or year. Wherever we seek the Lord with true hearts He is found by us; whenever we cry to Him He hears us.

You have here permission given to come to the mercy seat when you will, for the veil of the Most Holy place is rent in two from top to bottom, and our access to the mercy seat is undisputed and indisputable. The monarch whose palace was in Shushan would have none approach him unless he sent for them; but the King of kings has called for all His people, and they may come at all times. They were slain who went before the king Ahasuerus, unless he stretched out his scepter to them; but our King never withdraws His scepter, it is always stretched out, and whoever desires to come to Him may come now, and come at any time. Among the Persians there were some few of the nobility who had the peculiar and special right of an audience with the king at any time they chose. That peculiar right of a few and of the very great is the privilege of every child of God. He may come before the King at all times. The dead of night is not too late for God; the breaking of the morning, when the first gray light is seen, is not too early for the Most High; at midday He is not too busy; and when the evening gathers He is not too weary with His children's prayers. To pray continually is a most

> *Nothing can set a barrier between a praying soul and its God.*

sweet and precious permit to the believer to pour out his heart at all times before the Lord.

The doors of the temple of divine love shall not be shut. Nothing can set a barrier between a praying soul and its God. The road of angels and of prayers is ever open. Let us but send out the dove of prayer and we may be certain that she will return to us with an olive branch of peace in her mouth. Evermore the Lord has regard for the pleadings of His servants and waits to be gracious to them.

❦

Jesus, You opened the doors of the temple forever. May my heart always dwell there. Amen.

Your Will Be Done

———— ∞ ————

"Your will be done on earth as it is in heaven."
—MATTHEW 6:10

God knows what will best minister to His gracious designs. He ordains all things according to the counsel of His will, and that counsel never errs. Let us adoringly consent that it shall be so, desiring no alterations. That *will* may cost us dearly, yet let it never cross our wills. Let our minds be wholly submissive to the mind of God. That *will* may bring us bereavement, sickness, and loss, but let us learn to say, "He is the LORD; let him do what is good in his eyes" (1 Sam. 3:18). We should not only yield to

28

the divine will, but acquiesce in it so as to rejoice in the tribulations that it ordains. This is a high attainment, but we set ourselves to reach it. He who taught us this prayer used it Himself in the most unrestricted sense. When the bloody sweat stood on His face, and all fear and trembling of man in anguish were upon Him, He did not dispute the decree of the Father, but bowed His head and cried, "Not my will, but Yours be done."

It is a brave prayer that only a heaven-born faith can utter.

If the prayer had not been dictated by our Lord Jesus, we might think it too bold. Can it ever be that this earth, a mere drop of a bucket, should touch the great sea of life and light above and not be lost in it? Can it remain earth and yet be made like heaven? The earth that is subjected to vanity, defiled with sin, furrowed with sorrow, can holiness dwell in it as in heaven? Our Divine Instructor would not teach us to pray for impossibilities. He puts such petitions into our mouths as can be heard and answered. Yet it is a great prayer; it has the hue of the infinite about it. Can earth be tuned to the harmonies of heaven? It can be, and it must be, for He who taught us this prayer did not mock us with vain words. It is a brave prayer that only a heaven-born faith can utter. Yet it is not the offspring of presumption, for presumption never longs for the will of the Lord to be perfectly performed.

Up yonder there is no playing with sacred things: they do His commandments, hearkening to the voice of His word. Would that God's will were not alone preached and sung below, but actually done as it is in heaven.

Father, whatever Your will may cost me this day, it is far less than what it cost Your Son. May Your will be done. Amen.

The Throne of Grace

---✎✎✎---

Let us then approach the throne
of grace with confidence.
—HEBREWS 4:16

If I find myself favored by divine grace to stand among those favored ones who frequent God's courts, shall I not feel glad? I might have been in His prison, driven from His presence forever, but now I am before His throne, even invited into His secret chamber of gracious audience. Shall not my thankfulness ascend into joy, and shall I not feel that I am made recipient of great favors when I am permitted to pray?

My heart, be sure that you prostrate yourself in such a presence. If He is so great, place your mouth in the dust before Him, for He is the most powerful of all kings. His throne has sway in all worlds. Heaven obeys Him cheerfully, hell trembles at His frown, and earth is constrained to yield Him worship, willingly or unwillingly. His power can create or destroy. My soul, be sure that when you draw near to the Omnipotent, who is as a consuming fire, put your shoes from off your feet and worship Him with lowliest humility.

> *Heaven obeys Him cheerfully, hell trembles at His frown, and earth is constrained to yield Him worship.*

He is the most Holy of all kings. His throne is a great white throne—unspotted and clear as crystal. "The stars are not pure in his eyes, how much less…a son of man, who is only a worm!" (Job 25:5–6). With what lowliness should you draw near to Him. Familiarity there may be, but let it not be unhallowed. Boldness there should be, but let it not be impertinent. You are still on earth, and He in heaven. You are still a worm of the dust, and He the Everlasting. Before the mountains were brought forth, He was God, and if all created things should pass away, yet He would still be the same. I am afraid we do not bow as we should before the Eternal Majesty. Let us ask the Spirit of God to put us in a right frame, that every one of our prayers may be a reverential approach to the Infinite Majesty above.

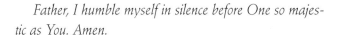

Father, I humble myself in silence before One so majestic as You. Amen.

Adoration

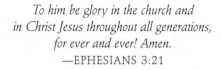

*To him be glory in the church and
in Christ Jesus throughout all generations,
for ever and ever! Amen.*
—EPHESIANS 3:21

In the text we find adoration; not prayer, the apostle Paul had done that. We find adoration—not even so much the act of praise as the full sense that praise is due, and far more of it than we can render. I hardly know how to describe adoration. Praise is a river flowing on joyously in its own channel, banked up on either side that it may run toward its one object. But adoration is the same river overflowing all banks, flooding the soul and covering the entire nature with its great waters; and these not so

much moving and stirring as standing still in pro-
found repose, mirroring the glory that shines down
upon it, like a summer's sun upon a sea of glass.
Adoration is not seeking the divine presence, but is
conscious of it to an unutterable
degree, and therefore full of awe and
peace, like the sea of Galilee when its
waves felt the touch of the sacred
feet. Adoration is the fullness, the
height and depth, the length and
breadth of praise. Adoration seems to
me to be as the starry heavens that
are always telling the glory of God,

> *Adoration is
> the eloquent
> silence of a
> soul that is
> too full for
> language.*

and yet "there is no speech or language where their
voice is not heard" (Ps. 19:3). It is the eloquent
silence of a soul that is too full for language. To
prostrate yourself in the dust in humility, and yet to
soar aloft in sublime thought; to sink into nothing,
and yet to be so enlarged as to be filled with all the
fullness of God; to have no thought and yet to be all
thought; to lose yourself in God; this is adoration.

We should set apart far longer time for this sacred
engagement. It is for our highest enrichment if we

made it our daily prayer that the blessed Spirit would frequently bear us right out of ourselves and lift us above all the small concerns that surround us, till we are only conscious of God and His exceeding glory. Oh that He would plunge us into the God-head's deepest sea till we are lost in His immensity and could only exclaim in wonder, "O the depths! O the depths!" Turn your eyes away from all else to Him, even to the Lord God Almighty and the Lamb. Consider Him only, and render Him glory.

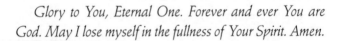

Glory to You, Eternal One. Forever and ever You are God. May I lose myself in the fullness of Your Spirit. Amen.

Prayer's Golden Key

———— ᘓᕀᘓ ————

*"Call to me and I will answer you
and tell you great and unsearchable
things you do not know."*
—JEREMIAH 33:3

Stones are broken only by an earnest use of the hammer, and the stone mason usually goes down on his knees. Use the hammer of diligence and let the knee of prayer be exercised. There is not a stony doctrine in Revelation that is profitable to you to understand that will not fly into pieces under the exercise of prayer and faith. "To have prayed well is to have studied well" was a wise sentence of Luther's. You may force your way through anything with the leverage of prayers. Thoughts and reasonings may be like the steel wedges that may open a way into truth, but prayer is the lever that forces open the iron chest of sacred mystery. The kingdom of heaven still suffers violence, and the violent take it by force. If you take care that you work away with the mighty implement of prayer, nothing can stand against you.

> *If you take care that you work away with the mighty implement of prayer, nothing can stand against you.*

The saint may expect to discover deeper experiences and to know more of the higher spiritual life by being much in prayer. Not all the developments of spiritual life are similarly easy to attain. There are the common frames of repentance and faith, but there is also an upper realm of rapture, communion, and conscious union with Christ. All believers see Christ, but not all believers put their fingers into the prints of the nails. Not all have the privilege of leaning upon Jesus' bosom or being caught up into the third heaven.

Most Christians are only up to their ankles in the river of experience. Some have waded till the stream is up to their knees. A few find the water up to their shoulders. But a very few find it a river to swim in— the bottom of which they cannot touch. There are heights in experiential knowledge of the things of God the eagle's eye of acumen and the philosophic thought has never seen. There are secret paths that the lion's cub of reason and judgment has not as yet learned to travel. God alone can bring us there, but the chariot in which He takes us up and the fiery steeds with which that chariot is dragged are prevailing prayers.

Lord Jesus, draw me deeper into the stream of Your love that I might know and glorify You more. Amen.

Prayer in a Cave

———— ✺✺✺ ————

A maskil of David.
When he was in the cave. A prayer.
—TITLE OF PSALM 142

David did pray when he was in the cave. If he had prayed half as much when he was in the palace as he did when he was in the cave, it would have been better for him. If he had been looking up to heaven, if his heart had been in communion with God, he might never have looked from the roof to the house and committed that great crime that so deeply stained his whole character.

Our God is not the God of the hills only, but of the valleys also; He is God of both sea and land. He heard Jonah when earth with her bars seemed to be about him forever. Wherever you work, you can pray. Wherever you lie, you can pray. There is no place to which you can be banished where God is not near, and there is no time of day or night when His throne is inaccessible. The caves have heard the best prayers. Some of God's people shine brightest in the dark. Many an heir of heaven never prays so well as when driven by necessity to pray. Some sing aloud upon a bed of sickness who are seldom heard from when they are well. Some ring God's high praises in the fire of affliction who did not praise Him before the trial came.

> *Some ring God's high praises in the fire of affliction who did not praise Him before the trial came.*

David was to be king over all Israel. What was the way to Jerusalem's throne? It was directed through the cave of Adullam. He must go there as an outcast, for that was the way by which he would be made king. Whenever God is about bring you to a higher platform of spiritual life, you always first get thrown down. He makes you hungry before He feeds you; He strips you before He clothes you; He makes nothing of you before he makes something of you. Jacob only became "the prince of God" after God touched his thigh and put it out of joint. Do not wonder, then, if you go by the way of the cave. Here it is that He will teach you to pray.

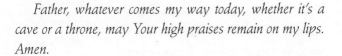

Father, whatever comes my way today, whether it's a cave or a throne, may Your high praises remain on my lips. Amen.

Prayers of the Moment

❦

Then I prayed to the God of heaven.
—NEHEMIAH 2:4

For four months Nehemiah had prayed about the ruined walls of Jerusalem. Day and night Jerusalem seemed written on his heart, painted on his eyeballs. With one single passion absorbing Nehemiah's soul, God sent Nehemiah an opportunity. King Artaxerxes' question of what Nehemiah wishes to do for Jerusalem is followed by an immediate prayer for help.

This was not the prayer that stands knocking at mercy's door, but it was the concentration of many knocks in one. It was introduced between the king's question and Nehemiah's answer. Probably the interval was not long enough to be noticed, but it was long enough for God to notice it—long enough for Nehemiah to have sought and obtained guidance from God as to how to answer the king. Nehemiah, being "very much afraid" at the moment, offered his prayer like an electric flash, like the winking of an eye. It was done intuitively, yet done it was, and it proved to be a prayer that prevailed with God.

> *Never underestimate the value of a prayer of the moment.*

We know that it was a silent prayer. Artaxerxes never knew that Nehemiah prayed, though he stood probably within a yard of him. In the innermost shrine of the temple—in the holy of holies of his own secret soul—there did he pray. Short and silent was the prayer. It was a prayer on the spot. He did not go to his chamber as Daniel did and open the window. Daniel was right, but this was a different occasion. He did not even turn his face to the wall. No, but there and then, with the king's cup in his hand, he prayed to the God of heaven, and then answered the king's question. And his prayer was very intense and very direct. "The God of heaven" was Nehemiah's favorite name for God. He knew whom he was praying to. He did not draw a bow and shoot his prayer in any direction, but he prayed straight to God for the thing he wanted.

Never underestimate the value of a prayer of the moment. Nehemiah's prayer—a little bit of a prayer pushed in sideways between a question and an answer, a mere fragment of devotion—was never erased from these words of biblical history.

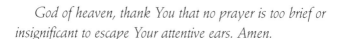

God of heaven, thank You that no prayer is too brief or insignificant to escape Your attentive ears. Amen.

Courageous Prayers

—❦—

*Now when Daniel learned that the decree
had been published, he went home to his upstairs
room where the windows opened toward Jerusalem. Three
times a day he got down on his knees and prayed, giving
thanks to his God, just as he had done before.*
—DANIEL 6:10

There are some forms of spiritual life that are not absolutely essential, but prayer is of the very essence of spirituality. He who has no prayer lacks the very breath of the life of God in the soul. Daniel, we are told, was a man of excellent spirit, a man abundant in prayer. He prayed for his people who were in exile, remembering those who were in bonds. He interceded for Jerusalem. It grieved him that the city was laid waste, that still the Chaldean destroyer was upon Mount Zion, so beautiful and once the joy of the whole earth. He pleaded for the return from the captivity, which he knew was ordained of his God. It would have been a delightful thing to have listened at the key hole of Daniel's closet and heard the mighty intercessions that went up to the Lord God of Hosts.

He who has no prayer lacks the very breath of the life of God in the soul.

With all his prayers we are told that Daniel mingled thanksgiving. It is poor devotion that is always asking and never returning its gratitude. Prayers in which there is no thanksgiving are selfish things and will not receive an answer. Prayer and praise resemble the process by which we live. Prayer takes in deep draughts of the love and grace of God, and then praise breathes it out again. Daniel offered to God that sweet incense that was made of many spices, of sincere desires and longings mingled with adoration.

Daniel had been exalted to very great worldly prosperity, but his soul had also prospered, refusing to be intoxicated by success or to turn aside to gather the golden apples. He sustained the energy of his outward profession by constant, secret communion with God. When his enemies assailed him, he knew there were more precious things than honor and wealth. Better an ounce of divine grace in prayer than a ton of worldly goods. To kneel to God's honor is worth whatever it may cost, even if it means the lion's den.

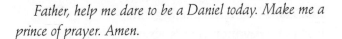

Father, help me dare to be a Daniel today. Make me a prince of prayer. Amen.

DAY 15

The Secret of
Power in Prayer

*If you remain in me and my words
remain in you, ask whatever you wish,
and it will be given you.*
—JOHN 15:7

Prayer comes spontaneously from those who
abide in Jesus. Prayer is the natural outgushing
of a soul in communion with Jesus. As the leaf and
fruit come out of the vine branch without any conscious effort and simply because of its living union
with the stem, so prayer buds and blossoms and
fruits out of souls abiding in Jesus. As stars shine, so
do abiders pray. They do not say to themselves, "It
is the time for us to get to our task and pray." No,

49

they pray as wise men eat—namely, when the desire
for it is upon them. They do not cry out as under
bondage, "We ought to be in
prayer, but I do not feel like it.
What a weariness it is!" They
have a glad errand at the mercy
seat and rejoice to go there.
Hearts abiding in Christ send
forth supplications as fires send
out flames and sparks. Souls
abiding in Jesus open the day with prayer; prayer
surrounds them as an atmosphere all day long; at
night they fall asleep in prayer. They are able joy-
fully to say, "When I awake, I am still with you" (Ps.
139:18). Habitual asking comes out of abiding in
Christ.

*Hearts abiding
in Christ send forth
supplications as
fires send out
flames and sparks.*

The fruit of our abiding also includes liberty in
prayer. Have you not been on your knees at times
without power to pray? Have you not felt that you
could not plead as you desired? You wanted to pray,
but the waters were frozen and would not flow. The
will was present, but not the freedom to present that
will in prayer. Do you, then, desire liberty in prayer

so that you may speak with God as a man speaks with his friend? Here is the way: "If you remain in me and my words remain in you, ask whatever you wish." I do not mean that you will gain liberty as to a mere fluency of words, for that is a very inferior gift. Fluency is a questionable endowment, especially when it is not accompanied with the weight of thought and depth of feeling. Some brethren pray by the yard, but true prayer is measured by weight— not by length. A single groan before God may have more fullness of prayer in it than a fine oration of great length.

Jesus, I want to abide in You today. To pray is my joy. Amen.

Intercessory Prayer

————⚬⚬⚬————

After Job had prayed for his friends,
the LORD made him prosperous again.
—JOB 42:10

What a promise is contained in this verse! Our longest sorrows have an ending, and there is a bottom to the profoundest depths of misery. Winter shall not frown forever; summer shall soon smile. The tide shall not eternally ebb out; the floods retrace their march. The night shall not hang its darkness forever over our souls; the sun shall yet arise with healing beneath his wings. He who turned the captivity of Job can turns yours as the streams in the south. He shall make your vineyard to blossom and your field to yield her fruit again.

Intercessory prayer was the sign of Job's returning greatness. It was the rainbow in the cloud and the dove bearing the olive branch. When Job's soul began to expand itself in holy and loving prayer for his erring brethren, the heart of God showed itself to him by returning his prosperity and cheering his soul within.

Remember that intercessory prayer is the sweetest prayer God ever hears. What wonders it has wrought! Intercessory prayer has stopped plagues. It removed the darkness that rested over Egypt, drove away the frogs that leaped upon the land, scattered the lice and locusts that plagued the inhabitants of Zoan, removed the thunder and lightning, stayed all the ravages that God's avenging hand did upon Pharaoh and his people. We know that intercessory prayer healed diseases in the early church. We have evidence of it in old Mosaic times. When Miriam was smitten with leprosy, Moses prayed

Intercessory prayer was the sign of Job's returning greatness. It was the rainbow in the cloud and the dove bearing the olive branch.

and the leprosy was removed. Intercessory prayer has raised the dead, for Elijah stretched himself upon the child seven times, and the child sneezed, and the child's soul returned. As to how many souls intercessory prayer has instrumentally saved, only eternity shall reveal it! There is nothing that intercessory prayer cannot do. Believer, you have a mighty engine in your hand—use it well, use it constantly, use it now with faith, and you shall surely prevail.

———∞∞∞———

Holy Spirit, shape my life until I truly become an intercessor for God. Amen.

Hindrances to Prayer

———∞∞∞———

...so that nothing will hinder your prayers.
—1 PETER 3:7

Prayer is a most precious thing, for it is the channel by which priceless blessings come to believers and the window through which their needs are supplied by a gracious God. Prayer is the vessel that trades with heaven and comes home from the celestial country laden with treasures of far greater worth than ever Spanish galleon brought from the land of gold. It is so invaluable that the danger of hindering it is used by Peter as a motive why—in marriage relationships and household concerns—husbands and wives should behave in such a way that their united prayers be not hindered. Anything that hinders prayer must be wrong. If anything regarding the family is injuring our power in prayer, there is an urgent demand for change. Husband and wife should pray together as joints heirs of grace, and any behavior or attitude or habit that hinders this is evil.

> *What you are upon your knees, you are really before your God.*

Prayer is the true gauge of spiritual power. To restrain prayer is a dangerous and deadly tendency. This is a faithful saying: What you are upon your knees, you are really before your God. What the Pharisee and the publican were in prayer was the true criterion of their spiritual state (Luke 18:10–14). You may maintain a decent repute among men, but it is a small matter to be judged of man's judgment, for men see only the surface, while the Lord's eyes pry into the recesses of the soul. If He sees that you are prayerless, He makes small account of your attendance at religious meetings or your loud spiritual words. If you are a man of earnest prayer—and especially if

the spirit of prayer is in you so that your heart habit-
ually talks with God—things are right with you. But
if this is not the case and your prayers are hindered,
there is something in your spiritual system that needs
to be ejected or something lacking that needs to be
supplied. "Guard your heart, for it is the wellspring
of life" (Prov. 4:23), and living prayers are among the
wellspring.

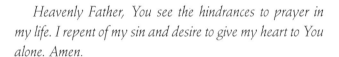

*Heavenly Father, You see the hindrances to prayer in
my life. I repent of my sin and desire to give my heart to You
alone. Amen.*

Fresh Visitations
of God

⸺∞⸺

*The LORD appeared to [Solomon] a second time, as he had
appeared to him at Gibeon. The LORD said to him: "I have
heard the prayer and plea you have made before me."*
—1 KINGS 9:2–3

No matter what level of spiritual maturity we
are on, we need renewed appearances, fresh
manifestations, new visitations from on high. While
it is right to thank God for the past and look back
with joy to His visits to you in your early days as a
believer, I encourage you to seek God for special visitations of His presence. I do no mean to minimize
our daily walk in the light of His countenance, but
consider that though the ocean has its high tides

twice every day, yet it also has its spring tides. The sun shines whether we see it or not, even through our winter's fog, and yet it has its summer brightness. If we walk with God constantly, there are special seasons when He opens the very secret of His heart to us and manifests Himself to us—not only as He does not to the world but also as He does not at all times to His own favored ones. Not every day in a palace is a banqueting day, and not all days with God are so clear and glorious as certain special sabbaths of the soul in which the Lord unveils His glory. Happy are we if we have once beheld His face, but happier still if He comes to us again in the fullness of favor.

Happy are we if we have once beheld His face, but happier still if He comes to us again in the fullness of favor.

I commend you to be seeking God's second appearances. We should be crying to God most pleadingly that He would speak to us a second time. We do not need to be converted again, but we do need the windows of heaven to be opened again and again over our heads. We need the Holy Spirit to be given again as at Pentecost and that we should renew our youth like the eagles, to run without weariness and walk without fainting. What the Lord spoke to Solomon concerned his prayer. And as the Lord answered Solomon's prayer in this second appearance, we may be sure that there was much about the prayer that makes it a model for us. We shall do well to pray after the manner that successful intercessors have set.

Holy Spirit, I need You every morning to renew my strength and soul. Visit me now, I pray. Amen.

The Gift Unspeakable

⊸⊷⊸

Thanks be to God for his indescribable gift!
—2 CORINTHIANS 9:15

Hold a theology that magnifies Christ as God's unspeakable gift. When a man gets to cutting down sin, paring down depravity, and making little of future punishment, let him no longer preach to you. Some whittle away the gospel to the small end of nothing. They make our divine Lord to be a sort of blessed nobody; they bring down salvation to mere salvability, make certainties into probabilities, and treat truth as mere opinion. When you see a preacher making the gospel small by degrees and miserably less, till there is not enough of it left to make soup for a sick grasshopper, leave. Christ is all; Christ is the unspeakable gift of God.

Let us vow today that, His grace helping us, we will praise Him for His unspeakable gift as long as we live.

We can never possibly thank Him as we ought. Who has ever worthily blessed the Lord on the account of salvation alone? If Jesus is our salvation, when should we thank God for Him? Why, every morning when we wake. How long should we continue? Till we go to sleep again. From the rising of the sun to the going down of the same His name is to be extolled. Let us praise God till sleep steeps our senses in a sweet forgetfulness. It is even pleasant to go on singing to the Lord in visions of our bed, as if the chords of grateful emotion vibrated after the hand of thought had ceased to play on them. It is good when even this wayward fancy of our dreams wanders toward the Beloved One, never rambling outside of holy ground. Let even our night dreams sing hymns to Jesus. Oh, to get into such a state that we shall be still praising Him, praising, and praising, and praising, and never ceasing. Let us give double praise while we can. Let us vow today that, His grace helping us, we will praise Him for His unspeakable gift as long as we live. We shall never get to an end of this holy work. Help us, all who know His salvation! Help us, angels! Help us, all you coming ages! Help us, all you stars of light! Yet still the thing shall be unspeakable even to the end. O Holy Spirit, write this line of gratitude upon the tablets of our hearts.

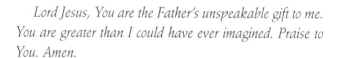

Lord Jesus, You are the Father's unspeakable gift to me. You are greater than I could have ever imagined. Praise to You. Amen.

Sweet to God

...golden bowls full of incense,
which are the prayers of the saints.
—REVELATION 5:8

The prayers the Lord accepts are not the chantings of functionaries, the litanies of priests, or the devout tones of an organ—they must be the prayers of the saints. In the believer's life, character, and soul, the sweetness lies. The acceptance comes not unless they are the prayers of the saints. And who are the saints? They are those whom the Lord has made holy by the power of His Spirit, whose nature He has purified, whom He has washed in the precious blood of Jesus and so sanctified unto

Himself, whom He has filled with His Spirit and so
set apart to His worship. They love Him, praise Him,
bow before Him with solemn awe, lift their whole
souls up in adoring love to Him. Their thoughts,
desires, longings, confessions, pleadings, and praises
are sweet to God. This is music to Him, perfume to
His heart, delight to His Infinite mind, and pleasant
to His sacred spirit, for "God is spirit,
and his worshipers must worship in
spirit and in truth" (John 4:24). After
no other fashion is a spiritual God to
be worshiped.

*Faith must
be a part
of the
fragrance
of prayer.*

In prayer, that which is sweet to
God is not the words used, though
they ought to be appropriate; but the
sweetness lies not in anything perceptible to the outward senses but in the secret qualities comparable to
the essence and aroma of sweet spices. In the incense
there lies a subtle and almost spiritual essence that is
drawn from it by the burning coals that causes the
latent sweetness to spread itself abroad till all around
confess its power. So it is in prayer. Our prayers may
be very beautiful in appearance and might appear to

be the very paragon of devotion, but unless there is a secret spiritual force in them, they are vain things; faith must be a part of the fragrance of prayer. When I hear a person pray, I am not able to tell whether he prays in faith or not, but God perceives the faith or the absence of it, and the prayer is received or rejected as the case may be.

Our God and Father, You see the depths of my soul. May my prayers be pleasing to You. Amen.

Our Heavenly Father

—∞—

"Our Father in heaven."
—MATTHEW 6:9

What is that spirit of a child—that sweet spirit that makes him recognize and love his father? I cannot tell you unless you are a child yourself, and then you will know. And what is "the Spirit of adoption, whereby we cry, Abba, Father" (Rom. 8:15 KJV)? I cannot tell you, but if you felt it, you will know it. It is a sweet compound of faith that knows God to be my Father, love that knows Him as my Father, joy that rejoices in Him as my Father, fear that trembles to disobey Him because He is my Father, and a confident affection and trustfulness that relies upon Him, and casts itself wholly upon Him, because it knows by the infallible witness of the Holy Spirit, that Jehovah, the God of earth and heaven, is the Father of my heart. Have you ever felt the spirit of adoption? There is nothing like it beneath the sky. Other than heaven itself there is nothing more blissful than to enjoy that spirit of adoption. When the wind of trouble is blowing, and waves of adversity are rising, and the ship is reeling to the rock, how sweet to say "My Father," and to believe that His strong hand is on the helm! There is music; there is eloquence; there is the very essence of heaven's own bliss in that word, "My Father," when said by us with an unfaltering tongue, through the inspiration of the Spirit of the living God.

Our prayers may be little broken things; we cannot put them together, but our Father, He hears us.

And so we come to Him. When I talk to my Father I am not afraid He will misunderstand me; if I put my words a little out of place He understands my meaning. When we are little children we babble at times; still our father understands. Our prayers may be little broken things; we cannot put them together, but our Father, He hears us. Oh, what a beginning is "Our Father," to a prayer full of faults, and a foolish prayer, perhaps, a prayer in which we are going to ask what we should not ask for! The Lord reads the meaning and the desires of our heart. Let us draw near to His throne as children coming to a father, and let us declare our needs and our sorrows in the language that the Holy Spirit teaches us.

———— ≈≈≈ ————

Holy Spirit, how is it possible to be so loved by our heavenly Father? I rejoice as a child of God. Amen.

All Night in Prayer

———∞∞∞———

Jesus went out to a mountainside to pray,
and spent the night praying to God.
—LUKE 6:12

Did Jesus not seek the mountain to avoid a public display? If we pray to be seen by men, we shall have our reward, and a pitiful reward it will be. We shall have the admiration of shallow fools, and nothing more. If our object in prayer is to obtain blessings from God, we must present our prayers unspoiled by human observation. Get alone with your God if you would move His arm. If you fast, do not give the appearance to men that you are fasting. If you plead personally with God, tell none of it. Take care that this is a secret between God and your own soul; then shall your Father reward you openly. But if you parade about like a Pharisee, to sound your trumpet in the corner of the streets, you shall go where the Pharisee has gone, where hypocrites feel forever the wrath of God.

Jesus, therefore, to prevent interruption, to give Himself the opportunity of pouring out His whole soul, and to avoid ostentation, sought the mountain. What a grand oratory for the Son of God! What walls should have been so suitable? What room would have worthily housed so mighty an intercessor? The Son of God most fittingly entered God's own glorious temple of nature when He would commune with heaven. Those giant hills and the long shadows cast by the moonlight were alone worthy to be His companions. No pomp of gorgeous ceremony can possibly have equaled the glory of nature's midnight

Jesus, therefore, to prevent interruption, to give Himself the opportunity of pouring out His whole soul, and to avoid ostentation, sought the mountain.

on the wild mountain's side, where the stars, like the eyes of God, looked down upon the worshiper and the winds seemed as though they would bear the burden of His sighs and tears upon their willing wings. Samson, in the temple of the Philistines, moving the giant pillars, is a mere dwarf compared with Jesus of Nazareth moving heaven and earth as He bows Himself alone in the great temple of Jehovah.

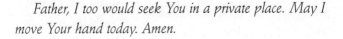

Father, I too would seek You in a private place. May I move Your hand today. Amen.

Legions of Angels

———⁓———

*"Put your sword back in its place.... Do you
think I cannot call on my Father, and he will at once put
at my disposal more than twelve legions of angels?"*
—MATTHEW 26:52–53

There can be no limit to the available resources
of the Christ of God. Thousands of thousands
of angels would fill the air if Jesus willed it. The
band that Judas led would be an insignificant squad
to be swallowed up at once if the Savior would but
summon His allies. Behold, the glory of our
betrayed and arrested Lord. If He was such then,
what is He now, when all power is given Him of His
Father! Bear in your mind the clear idea that Jesus in
His humiliation was nevertheless Lord of all things,

and especially of the unseen world, and of the armies that people it. The more clearly you perceive this, the more you will admire the all-conquering love that took Jesus to the death of the cross.

> You have but to pray to God, and angels shall bear you up in their hands lest you dash your foot against a stone.

Tarry here just a minute to recollect that the angels also are, according to your measure and degree, at your call. You have but to pray to God, and angels shall bear you up in their hands lest you dash your foot against a stone. We do not think enough of these heavenly beings, yet they are all ministering spirits sent forth to minister to those who are heirs of salvation. Like Elijah's servant, if your eyes were opened, you would see the mountain full of horses of fire and chariots of fire round about the servants of God. Let us learn from our Master to reckon upon forces invisible. Let us not trust in that which is seen of the eye and heard of the ear, but let us have respect to spiritual agencies that evade the senses but are known to faith. Angels play a far greater part in the affairs of Providence than we realize. God can raise us up friends on earth, and if He does not do so, He can find us abler friends in heaven. There is no need to pluck out the sword with which to cut off men's ears, for infinitely better agencies will work for us. Have faith in God, and all things shall work for your good. The angels of God think it an honor and a delight to protect the least of His children.

Lord Jesus, You are exalted at the Father's right hand. Nothing is too hard for You today. Amen.

Seeking Faith

-----∞∞∞-----

"Unless you people see miraculous signs and wonders,"
Jesus told him, "you will never believe." The royal official
said, "Sir, come down before my child dies."
—JOHN 4:48–49

Notice in the royal official's case that seeking
faith did not simply make him earnest in
prayer but made him persistent in prayer. He asked
once, and the only answer he received was an appar-
ent rebuff. He did not turn away in a sulk. No. "Sir,"
he said, "come down." I cannot tell you how he said
it, but I have no doubt it was expressed in soul-
moving terms, with tears starting from his eyes and
hands placed together in the attitude of entreaty. He
seemed to say, "I cannot let you go unless you come

76

and save my child. Please, do come. Is there anything I can say that can get you to come? Let a father's affection be my best argument. If my lips are not eloquent, let the tears of my eyes supply the place of the words of my tongue."

What mighty prayers are those that seeking faith will make a person pray!

What mighty prayers are those that seeking faith will make a person pray! I have heard the seeker sometimes plead with God with all the power that Jacob ever could have had at Jabbok's brook (Gen. 32:24–32). I have seen the sinner under distress of soul seem to take hold of the pillars of the gate of mercy and rock them to and fro as though he would sooner pull them up from their deep foundations than go away without effecting an entrance. I have seen sinners pull and tug, strive and fight and wrestle, rather than not enter the kingdom of heaven. No wonder that those who come before God with cold prayers do not find peace. Heat them red hot in the furnace of desire and they will burn their way upward to heaven. Those who merely say in the chill form of orthodoxy, "God be merciful to me a sinner," will never find mercy. It is the person who cries in the burning anguish of heartfelt emotion, "God be merciful to *me* a sinner! Save *me* or I perish!" who gains his plea. It is the person who concentrates his soul in every word and flings the violence of his being into every sentence that wins his way through the gates of heaven. Seeking faith can make a person do this.

Holy Ghost, stir in my heart and heat my prayers to red hot. May the pillars of mercy be shaken today. Amen.

The Generous Giver

———❦———

If any of you lacks wisdom, he should
ask God, who gives generously to all without
finding fault, and it will be given to him.
—JAMES 1:5

God does not give as we do, a mere handout to the beggar, but He gives His wealth by hand-fuls. Solomon asked for wisdom; God gave him wealth and power. In nearly every instance of prayer in the Old Testament, God gives ten times as much as is asked for. The Lord will "do immeasurably more than all we ask or imagine" (Eph. 3:20). This is the divine habit. He not only redeems His promises, but when He might meet them in silver He prefers to pay them in gold. He is exceedingly generous. Do you think He will begin to be stingy with you? If He should generously forgive your sins, He will be none the poorer; if He should withhold forgiveness, He will be none the richer. Why should He withhold His favor? You want to wash away your sins; there is a river of grace to wash in. You want grace to refresh your souls; He has floods to pour upon the dry ground. We read of the unsearchable riches of Christ. Ho! you leviathan sinners, here is an ocean of mercy for you to swim in. Ho! you elephantine sinners, here is an ark large enough to hold you and float you above the waters of the deluge! You whose sins of pride reach up to heaven and whose feet of lust are plunged into the mire of hell, the sacred hiding place is large enough to hide even you. The Lord is great in mercy. Who would not ask so generous a God?

> *God gives generously and does not dim the luster of His grace by finding fault with the seeker.*

God gives generously and does not dim the luster of His grace by finding fault with the seeker. This is a sweet word. He invited you to ask of Him wisdom, and He says he will give it to you. Will you add to all your others sins the sin of thinking that God would lie? Doubt not the Lord, distrust not the truthfulness of Jehovah, but come at once humbly, reverently, to the foot of the Savior's cross. View Him lifted on high, as the great atoning sacrifice; look to His streaming wounds; behold His brow still covered with the crimson drops that flow from the wounds caused by His thorny crown. Look to Him and live. There's life in a look at the Crucified One. Look to Him, and find in Him all you need.

Lord God, enlarge my vision of Your Son and of Your immense generosity. Drive out my doubts and fears. Amen.

He Is Able

————— ✥ —————

Now to him who is able to do immeasurably
more than all we ask or imagine, according to
his power that is at work within us…
—EPHESIANS 3:20

Perhaps you feel that you have in times of holy boldness and sacred access asked large things of God, such as one could only ask of the Great King: and yet your asking has been too short a line to reach the bottom of divine ability. Our prayer at its best and boldest has many a boundary. It is limited often by our sense of need; we barely know what we want; we need to be taught what we should pray for, or we never ask correctly. We mistake our spiritual condition, our soul's hunger is not keen enough, sin has taken the edge from our spiritual appetite, and therefore we cramp our prayers. But, blessed be God, He is not limited by our sense of need. His guest may ask for bread and water, but behold the feast He prepares.

Is there a single promise of God that any child of God perfectly understands? There is a meaning in the promises, a breadth, a length, a height, a depth, not compassed yet. God condescends to use human language, and to us the words mean silver, but He uses them in a golden sense. He never means less than He says, but He always means far more than we think He says. For this let us magnify the Lord. His power to bless is not bounded by our power to understand the blessing.

God is not limited by our sense of need. His guest may ask for bread and water, but behold the feast He prepares.

The promise here is emphatically that He is able to do above *all* that we think. Put together all that you have ever asked for. Heap it up, and then pile upon the top all that you have ever thought of concerning the riches of divine grace. What a mountain!

Here we have hill on hill, as though Alp on Alp were heaped on end to build a staircase or a Jacob's ladder to the very stars. Go on! Go on! It is no Babel tower you build, and yet its top will not reach to heaven. High as this pyramid of prayers may be piled, God's ability to bless is higher still. Above all the blessings that can be imagined that are useful and beneficial to us, He is able to do above it.

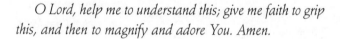

O Lord, help me to understand this; give me faith to grip this, and then to magnify and adore You. Amen.

DAY 27

Hope

—∞∞—

"Bring the boy here to me."
—MATTHEW 17:17

Prayer and fasting are prescribed by the Lord as the means of joining us to greater power than we should otherwise possess, and the church of God would be far stronger to wrestle with this ungodly age if she were more given to these means. Prayer links us to heaven; fasting separates us from earth. Prayer takes us into the banqueting house of God; fasting delivers the soul from being encumbered with the fullness of bread that perishes. When believers bring themselves up to the uttermost possibilities of

85

spiritual vigor, then they will be able, by God's Spirit working in them, to cast out devils that would otherwise laugh them to scorn. But for all that, there will still remain those mountainous difficulties that must be directly brought to the Master's personal agency for help.

All hell confesses the majesty of His power and the splendor of His Godhead.

Let me beg you to remember that Jesus Christ is still alive. Simple as that truth is, you need to be reminded of it. We very often estimate the power of the church by looking at her ministers and members, but the power of the church does not lie here, it lies in the Holy Spirit, and in an ever living Savior. Jesus lives today as He did when that anxious father brought his son to Jesus. We have neither the power to work natural miracles or spiritual miracles. Christ has the power to work any kind of wonder, and He is still willing and able to work spiritual miracles. I delight to think of my living Christ to whom I may bring every difficulty that occurs in my own soul and in the souls of others.

Remember, too, that Jesus lives in the place of authority. All hell confesses the majesty of His power and the splendor of His Godhead. There is no demon, however strong, who will not tremble before Him, and Jesus is the master of hearts and consciences. There cannot be a case too hard for Him. Is Christ unable to save, or are there diseases too many for the Great Physician to heal? Never can it be. Christ outdone by Satan and by sin? Impossible. He breaks the bars of iron and the gates of brass asunder that captives might be brought forth to liberty.

━━━━∞━━━━

Jesus Christ, You are greater than anything I will ever face. I fall into Your arms and live in Your mercy. Amen.

The Cure for Care

—◆◆◆—

Do not be anxious about anything,
but in everything, by prayer and petition, with
thanksgiving, present your requests to God. And the
peace of God, which transcends all understanding, will
guard your hearts and your minds in Christ Jesus.
—PHILIPPIANS 4:6–7

Why allow care to keep gnawing at your heart? It weakens our power to help ourselves, and especially our power to glorify God. A care-full heart hinders us from seeing anything clearly. It is like taking a telescope, breathing on it with the hot breath of our anxiety, putting it to our eye, and then saying that we cannot see anything but clouds. Of course we cannot, and we never shall as long as we breathe upon it. If we are calm, quiet, self-possessed, we should do the right thing. We should be "all there" in the time of difficulty. That man may expect to have presence of mind who has the presence of God. If we forget to pray, do we wonder that we are all in a worry and do the first thing that occurs to us—which is generally the worst thing—instead of waiting till we see what should be done and then trustfully and believingly doing it as in the sight of God? Care is harmful.

That man may expect to have presence of mind who has the presence of God.

I suppose it is true for many of us that our cares are manifold. If you are like me, once you become careful, anxious, fretful, you are never able to count your cares, even though you might count the hairs of your head. Cares multiply to those who are care-full. When you are as full of cares as you think you can be, you will be sure to find another crop of cares growing up all around you. The indulgence of this habit of anxiety leads to its getting dominion over life till life is not worth living by reason of the care we have about it. Cares and worries are manifold; therefore let your prayers be manifold. Turn everything that is a care into a prayer. Let your cares be the raw material of your prayers. As the alchemist hoped to turn dross into gold, you have the power to actually turn what naturally would have been a care into a spiritual treasure in the form of prayer. Baptize every anxiety into the name of the Father, the Son, and the Holy Spirit, and so make it into a blessing.

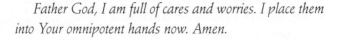

Father God, I am full of cares and worries. I place them into Your omnipotent hands now. Amen.

The Conditions of Power in Prayer

————∞∞∞————

*We have confidence before God and receive
from him anything we ask, because we obey
his commands and do what pleases him.*
—1 JOHN 3:21–22

Childlike confidence makes us pray as none else can. It causes a man to pray for great things that he would never have asked for if he had not learned this confidence. It also causes him to pray for little things that many people are afraid to ask for, because they have not yet felt toward God the confidence of children. I have often felt that it requires more confidence in God to pray to Him about a little thing than about great things. We imagine that our great things are somehow worthy of God's attention, though in truth they are little enough to Him. And then we think that our little things must be so insignificant that it is an insult to bring them before Him.

What were mothers and fathers made for but to look after the small concerns of little children?

We need to realize that what is very important to a child may be very small to his parent, and yet the parent measures the thing not from his own point of view but from the child's. You heard your little boy the other day crying bitterly. The cause of the pain was a splinter in his finger. While you did not call in three surgeons to extract it, the splinter was a great thing to that little sufferer. Standing there with eyes all wet through tears of anguish, it never occurred to that boy that his pain was too small a thing for you to care about. What were mothers and fathers made for but to look after the small concerns of little children?

And God our Father is a good father who pities us as fathers pity their children. He counts the stars and calls them all by name, yet He heals the broken in heart and binds up their wounds. If you put your confidence in God, you will take your great things and little things to Him, knowing He will never belie your confidence.

———

Father, I come as a child to thank You that I know Your heart toward me. I love You. Amen.

DAY 30

Unanswered Prayer

———⁂———

O my God, I cry out by day, but you
do not answer, by night, and am not silent.
Yet you are enthroned as the Holy One.
—PSALM 22:2–3

N ever be tempted to give up your hold upon your only strength, upon your solitary hope. Under no conceivable circumstances ever give place for an instant to the dark thought that God is not true and faithful to His promises. Though a prayer is unanswered for seven years, say to the Lord, "still You are enthroned as the Holy One." Settle that in your mind. Never allow the faintest breath of suspicion to come upon the fame of the Most High, for He never warrants it. He is true; He is faithful. In this

94

apparently worst of all cases, He did finally deliver His Son and come to the rescue in due time. You may not know why He deals with you so strangely, but never think that He is unfaithful for an instant.

Never cease your prayers. No time is wrong for prayer. The glare of daylight should not tempt you to cease, and the gloom of midnight should not make you stop your cries. One of Satan's chief objects is to get the believer to put away the weapon of all-prayer. As long as we continue to cry to the Most High, Satan knows he cannot devour the very weakest lamb of the flock. Prayer, mighty prayer, will yet prevail if it has but time.

Prayer, mighty prayer, will yet prevail if it has but time.

Let your faith be still more resolved to give up all dependence anywhere but upon God, and let your cry grow more and more vehement. It is not every knock at mercy's door that will open it. He who would prevail must handle the knocker well, and dash it down again, and again, and again. As the old Puritan says, "Cold prayers ask for a denial, but it is red-hot prayers which prevail." Bring your prayers as some ancient battering ram against the gate of heaven and force it open with a sacred violence. The whole army of your soul must come into the conflict, and you must besiege the mercy seat, determined to win the day, and then you shall prevail. If there are delays, take them as good and sound advice to be more firm in your faith and more fervent in your cry.

———❧———

Lord Jesus, even the cross of Calvary could not prevent the final victory of resurrection. With that confidence I pray. Amen.